S. HRG. 114–730

GENERIC DRUG USER FEE AMENDMENTS: ACCELERATING PATIENT ACCESS TO GENERIC DRUGS

HEARING

OF THE

COMMITTEE ON HEALTH, EDUCATION, LABOR, AND PENSIONS

UNITED STATES SENATE

ONE HUNDRED FOURTEENTH CONGRESS

SECOND SESSION

ON

EXAMINING GENERIC DRUG USER FEE AMENDMENTS, FOCUSING ON
ACCELERATING PATIENT ACCESS TO GENERIC DRUGS

JANUARY 28, 2016

Printed for the use of the Committee on Health, Education, Labor, and Pensions

Available via the World Wide Web: http://www.gpo.gov/fdsys/

U.S. GOVERNMENT PUBLISHING OFFICE

98–472 PDF   WASHINGTON : 2018

For sale by the Superintendent of Documents, U.S. Government Publishing Office
Internet: bookstore.gpo.gov   Phone: toll free (866) 512–1800; DC area (202) 512–1800
Fax: (202) 512–2104   Mail: Stop IDCC, Washington, DC 20402–0001

CONTENTS

GENERIC DRUG USER FEE AMENDMENTS: ACCELERATING PATIENT ACCESS TO GENERIC DRUGS

THURSDAY, JANUARY 28, 2016

U.S. SENATE,
COMMITTEE ON HEALTH, EDUCATION, LABOR, AND PENSIONS,
Washington, DC.

The committee met, pursuant to notice, at 10:05 a.m. in room SD–430, Dirksen Senate Office Building, Hon. Lamar Alexander, chairman of the committee, presiding.

Present: Senators Alexander, Murray, Collins, Hatch, Roberts, Cassidy, Casey, Franken, Whitehouse, Murphy, and Warren.

OPENING STATEMENT OF SENATOR ALEXANDER

The CHAIRMAN. The Senate Committee on Health, Education, Labor, and Pensions will please come to order.

Senator Murray and I will each have an opening statement. Then, we will introduce our panel. And after witness testimony, we will each have 5 minutes of questions.

In December, President Obama signed into law the Every Student Succeeds Act, which proves our committee can work on difficult issues successfully. But a law that is not properly implemented is not worth the paper it is written on, which is why we are going to have strong oversight on that law and why we are having this hearing today, because we are here for the similar purpose of conducting oversight on the 2012 Generic Drug User Fee Amendments for the Food and Drug Administration Act. Specifically, those are the fees that are negotiated between the FDA and the generic drug makers to give the agency additional resources intended to speed the review of safe and effective generic drugs.

This is the first oversight hearing since those amendments were passed in 2012. It comes at a crucial time. Since 2012, the FDA has received nearly $1 billion in user fees, and performance does not seem to be living up to Congress or the patient's expectations, as the number of generic drugs approved each year remains about the same. The user fee agreements are due to be reauthorized next year, and so now seems to be a good time to take a look at what has happened.

The Generic Drug Program is a success story I think anyone would have to say. It was started 30 years ago by one of our committee members Senator Hatch and Representative Henry Waxman. It has increased competition and lowered drug prices. The program was created to make it easier for generic drugs to come in. Generic drugs, of course, are those drugs that are allowed to come into the market after a drug manufacturer's patent expires over a period of time.

Generic drugs have to have FDA approval also, but they do not have to have full clinical trials, and so a lot of expense is avoided. As a result, more generic drugs on the market create competition and lower prices for consumers. Over the last 30 years, what we have seen is that, today, now, 88 percent of prescription drugs purchased in the United States are generic drugs. Thirty years ago, that number was zero.

However, in 2012, 26 years after the first law passed, it became clear the drug approval program needed an overhaul. More generic drugs were coming from overseas. Companies in China and India were inspected less frequently than American companies. This put patients at risk and companies at a disadvantage.

There is a backlog of 4,700 applications waiting to be reviewed, and the median approval time to get review of the generic drug was 30 months. That far surpasses the 180-day timeframe for review that was laid out in the Hatch-Waxman amendments in 1984. And additionally, in 2012, many generic sterile injectable drugs were in shortage, causing doctors and hospitals to scramble to ensure patients were getting the best treatment possible.

So Congress passed these amendments in 2012. The idea is based upon similar agreements with other manufacturers and the FDA. Congress anticipated that (1) generic drug facilities abroad would be brought to the same standards as facilities in the U.S.; and (2) that American patients would benefit from faster approval of generic drugs, and those two actions together would create more competition and lower the price for the drugs.

But as I mentioned, in 2012, there was a backlog of 4,700 pending applications, and the information we have shows that that has dropped to 3,500 applications. The HHS inspector general has reported that the FDA is improving its inspections abroad, but the troubling news is that it seems to take FDA longer to get generic drugs through the approval process. The median approval times have slowed from 30 to 48 months, and the original number hoped for was 180 days.

As we discuss these issues today, I think it is important to keep in mind that drug pricing is a legitimate, real concern of Americans, but it is part of a larger concern of rising health care costs. The Congressional Budget Office announced this week that Federal spending for the major health programs—Medicare, Medicaid, ET cetera—represents the largest fraction of the projected growth and mandatory spending in 2016.

Two, while we are lowering prices, we want to make sure we continue to invest in and incentivize the development of lifesaving therapies. Congress has responded to that, Senator Murray's leadership and Senator Blunt especially, adding $2 billion to the appropriation process for NIH. That is $32 billion now for NIH in a year, but the pharmaceutical manufacturers spend $50 billion in a year coming up with new cures and treatments.

And three, to try to balance restraining the growth of drug prices and encouraging investment and incentives for lifesaving therapies, we need to avoid unnecessary regulatory burdens that drive up costs, and we need to do our best to keep the marketplace competitive.

For the last year, we have been working in a bipartisan way on ways to avoid unnecessary regulatory burdens. In the Aging Committee, Senator Collins and Senator McCaskill have been examining what improvements may be necessary to ensure that the FDA expedites applications for generic drugs to keep the marketplace competitive and drug prices down.

But still, over the last 30 years, this is a success story. Generic drugs have gone from 0 to 88 percent of the marketplace. It is hard to imagine what the prescription drug market today would look like without them. I look forward to the testimony today.

Senator Murray.

OPENING STATEMENT OF SENATOR MURRAY

Senator MURRAY. Thank you very much, Chairman Alexander, Director Woodcock. Thank you so much for being here, taking the time to be here, and for all your work on behalf of our families and our communities.

I am really glad that we have the opportunity today to talk about the FDA's Generic Drug Program. This is a program that is absolutely critical to helping patients get safe, affordable, high-quality treatments more quickly. Generic drug user fees have significantly improved the FDA's ability to keep up with the large volume of generic drug applications, and it has helped build on the important work done in Hatch-Waxman to both incentivize innovation and expand families' access to the best treatments and cures available.

There is, of course, room for improvement. While it was certainly a big undertaking to establish this program on an aggressive timeline, I hope that going forward we can encourage more communication and efficiency.

It is important to remember that both Hatch-Waxman and FDA programs like GDUFA are the result of strong bipartisan work. And as we move forward, the reauthorization of the Generic Drug User Fee Program next year, it is critical that our committee's tradition of bipartisanship on these issues continue.

I am looking forward to working with the Chairman and all of our colleagues to ensure the FDA has the tools and resources it needs to serve families and communities safely and effectively.

Today's hearing is also an important opportunity to talk about the related larger issue of prescription drug access and affordability in our country. Nearly half of our country's population and the vast majority of our seniors take prescription drugs. But families across the country have made clear that paying for prescription drugs is an increasingly unsustainable burden.

Nationwide, spending on prescription drugs was nearly $374 billion in 2014. That is an increase of roughly 13 percent in just 1 year. And we expect to see continued cost growth, so we need to face up to some tough questions. For instance, how can we continue to afford to make critical new treatments widely accessible to patients who need them?

Sadly, the status quo is working all too well for some bad actors at the very top, and they are doing everything but putting patients first. When someone like Martin Shkreli comes along to rig the system in favor of his profits above access without regard to research investments or patients' outcomes, we need to act.

We are on the cusp of major breakthroughs in personalized medicine, and there is real momentum around tackling some of the greatest medical challenges of our time like cancer and Alzheimer's. And we have to ask ourselves how we are going to guarantee that we have the research, the market, and the access to make sure the benefits from that lifesaving progress are felt across the system as a whole.

We also have to make sure that insurers are covering their fair share. We made important progress capping out-of-pocket spending as part of the Affordable Care Act, but there is more work to do to ensure that patients are not being saddled with too heavy a cost burden. And I am especially concerned that we must prevent carriers from discriminating against patients with the most expensive illnesses.

In addition, if our goal is to make sure patients have access to and can afford the best, safest, most effective cures and treatments, we have to consider the resources we are putting into this effort because the truth is we simply cannot realize the goal of access, quality, and affordability without the FDA and the NIH at full throttle.

If you want the FDA to be able to approve drugs more quickly without rolling back the gold standard of consumer safety and protection, then the FDA is going to need more support to do its job. And if you want the NIH to be able to drive innovation that delivers on so many patients' and families' hopes, that is also going to require sustained investment.

I was pleased that Democrats and Republicans were able to come together to boost support for the NIH through the spending bill last year, but I see no reason to stop there. In fact, as I have made clear, I believe as part of our committee's effort to advance medical innovation for families, it is critical that we increase mandatory funding for the FDA and for NIH. And I hope that is something we can continue to work on together.

As we look for ways to improve health care for families, making sure that prescription drugs are accessible and affordable has to be a top priority. Finding solutions will not be easy. These are challenges that cannot be ignored. And I am confident if we all come to the table ready to join together toward the common goal of ensuring our health care system works for families and puts their needs first, we can make real progress and deliver results that so many families and communities are waiting for.

Thank you, Mr. Chairman.

The CHAIRMAN. Thank you, Senator Murray.

I am pleased to welcome Dr. Janet Woodcock as our witness for today's hearing. Thanks, Dr. Woodcock, for being here. We know you are very busy running that important center at the FDA. Dr. Woodcock has been director of the Center for Drug Evaluation and Research at FDA, which performs the critical task of ensuring safe and effective drugs are available to improve the health of Americans.

She has been at the FDA about as long as we have known generic drug approval, about 30 years, and she has led many of the

FDA drug initiatives, including the Critical Path Initiative. She has been the Center's director since Congress passed the Generic Drug User Fee Amendments in 2012, so she is the leading expert on this program.

Dr. Woodcock, we thank you for coming and look forward to your testimony. If you can summarize it in about 5 minutes, you have several Senators here who would like to have a conversation with you about your testimony.

STATEMENT OF JANET WOODCOCK, M.D., DIRECTOR, CENTER FOR DRUG EVALUATION AND RESEARCH, FOOD AND DRUG ADMINISTRATION, SILVER SPRING, MD

Dr. WOODCOCK. Thank you, Mr. Chairman, Ranking Member, members of the committee. I am very pleased to be here to talk about this important issue.

The Hatch-Waxman legislation that established a Generic Drug Program has been extraordinarily successful for the public. As Chairman Alexander said, about 88 percent of dispensed prescriptions right now are generic. It is estimated it has saved the public $1.7 trillion.

In the last decade, the generic drug industry, being very successful, grew very rapidly, and it also globalizes manufacturing, making drugs all around the world. FDA's Generic Drug Review Program, in contrast, did not grow significantly, and we fell behind in both review and inspection capacity, and a backlog accrued and began to buildup of pending applications.

In response to this, in 2012, Congress enacted GDUFA reflecting a negotiated agreement between the industry and the FDA to address this and modernize the program. GDUFA is a 5-year program during which industry would pay $300 million a year in fees for service, and FDA would attempt to meet a progressively more difficult series of performance measures that have to do with the review, but many other activities as well that are summarized in my testimony.

In the 3 years since this was enacted, FDA has met and in many cases exceeded all the GDUFA performance goals that have been established. This has been a formidable task. In these 3 years, we have been managing over 6,000 generic drug applications, about 2,500 that were piled up at the start of the program that we had not gotten to and then almost 3,000 that were submitted since that time, far exceeding expectations for the number of applications that would be submitted each year.

Over 90 percent of all these applications have received some review by the FDA at this point, 90 percent of the 6,000. They have received some kind of communication also, and over 1,700 have been approved or tentatively approved. We tentatively approve when we cannot approve yet because patent is still blocking a full approval.

Last month alone, we approved or tentatively approved 99 generic drug applications. How this was accomplished is detailed in my written testimony. It is a very complicated picture. It required us to rebuild the entire program from the ground up. But none of this could have been done without the incredible dedication and passion of a lot of people at the FDA. I will tell you, Mr. Chairman and Ranking Member, that the people at FDA share your passion for ensuring that the families and communities in this country have access to affordable drugs where at all possible.

I would really like to publicly thank all the people who worked so hard and so long over the past 3 years to make this program work. It has been an incredible effort. The staff in the Office of Generic Drugs, who have worked extensively long hours over time, continued, got the job done; the staff in the newly formed Office of Pharmaceutical Quality that has totally revamped how we do the quality review; the staff in the Office of Regulatory Affairs, which is our field organization that not only has ramped up and hired and done more inspections but actually volunteered and helped do some of the review work so we could get these applications reviewed; and all the other people who pitched in. And we had people in our laboratories and ORA laboratories who put aside their experiments, who put their experiments on hold so they could review parts of generic drug applications that were qualified to review.

The heroic staff, who really launched our new informatics platform, we all know the story about government IT, huge IT implementation. It is never pretty. And we had multiple legacy systems. All the data had to be transformed and cleaned up and put into a single system. And we were in the depths of despair a few times, but we have gotten through that. We are running off a new IT system. It has already proven its worth, and I thank them because they really went through a lot.

The financial staff, who had to set up a fee collection system from scratch and collect all these fees and allocate them appropriately; and our HR and admin staff, who helped us hire over 1,000 people, more people to get this job done, we would not have done it without all of them. And I think we owe them a great deal of thanks for making this program work.

Now, discussions about the backlog and so forth I would like to have in our back-and-forth conversation because this is a complicated issue, but I think the news is good news. It is not bad news. And I recognize that there remain a number of challenges that we all need to address collectively, but I am really sure because we have gotten through the worst of this that we can deal with the challenges we have ahead.

I really look forward to your questions. Thank you.

[The prepared statement of Dr. Woodcock follows:]

PREPARED STATEMENT OF JANET WOODCOCK, M.D.

INTRODUCTION

Chairman Alexander, Ranking Member Murray and members of the committee, I am Dr. Janet Woodcock, Director of the Center for Drug Evaluation and Research (CDER) at the Food and Drug Administration (FDA or the Agency), which is part of the Department of Health and Human Services (HHS). Thank you for the opportunity to be here today to discuss FDA's implementation of the Generic Drug User Fee Amendments of 2012 (GDUFA).

Historically, the generic drug program has been a great success.

The generic drug industry has grown from modest beginnings into a major force in health care. According to the IMS Institute for Healthcare Informatics, generic drugs now account for 88 percent of prescriptions dispensed in the United States, and saved the U.S. health system $1.68 trillion from 2005 to 2014.

Chart 1. Generic Substitution and Annual Savings[1]

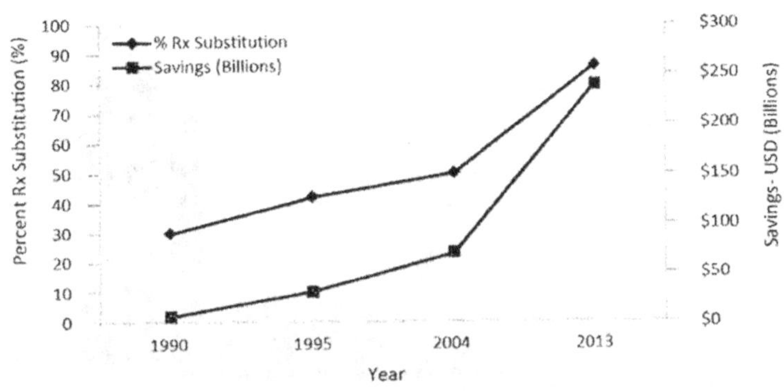

1. Annual generic utilization and savings data compiled from IMS Health, the Generic Pharmaceutical Association, and the Congressional Budget Office

This success brought new challenges.

Over the last several decades, the generic industry, the number of generic drug applications (known as "Abbreviated New Drug Applications" or "ANDAs") submitted to FDA for review, and the number of foreign facilities making generic drugs grew substantially. As a result, FDA's generic drug program became increasingly under-resourced. Its staffing did not keep pace with the growth of the industry.

Chart 2. Number of ANDAs Submitted Per Year and Number of Staff Over Time

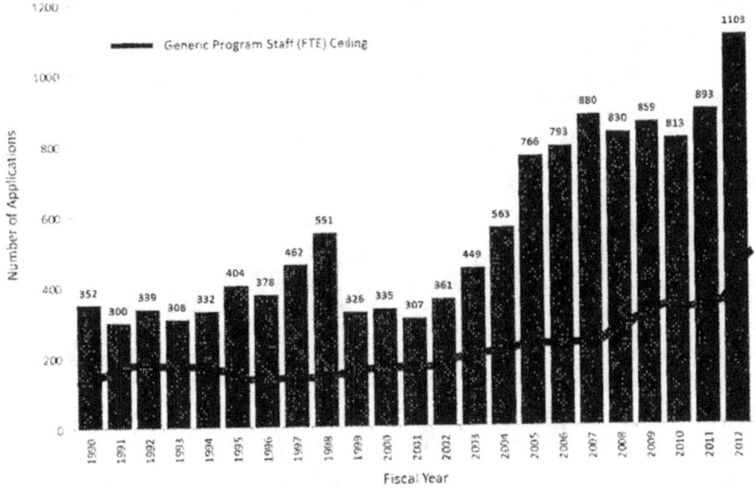

Because the program could not keep up with its workload, a backlog of submitted ANDAs developed and grew. It overwhelmed the FDA staff and created unpredictability and delay for industry.

Chart 3. ANDAs Pending Over 180 Days

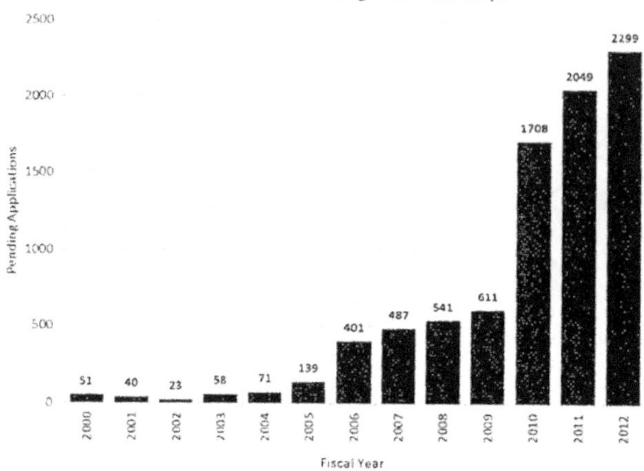

SOLUTION: GDUFA

After multiple attempts, FDA and the generic industry developed a proposal for a generic drug user fee program and submitted it to Congress. Congress enacted it as part of the Food and Drug Administration Safety and Innovation Act of 2012.

Under GDUFA, industry agreed to pay approximately $300 million in fees each year of the 5 year program. In exchange, FDA committed to performance goals, the specifics of which are contained in the Generic Drug User Fee Act Program Performance Goals and Procedures agreement that was negotiated with industry ("GDUFA Commitment Letter")[1]. Because of the amount of hiring, restructuring, and catch-up needed, performance goals were set to commence in the later years of the program. The GDUFA performance goals with respect to ANDAs, amendments to ANDAs, and prior approval supplements (PAS)[2] are timeframes by which FDA is to take a "first action" on an application, by either granting an approval or tentative approval,[3] or, if there are deficiencies that prevent approval, identifying those deficiencies to the applicant in a complete response letter or in a refusal to receive[4] the application. When deficiencies are identified, industry usually responds by correcting them and resubmitting the application.

Chart 4. Major GDUFA Performance Goals**

Goals	Fiscal year 2015	Fiscal year 2016	Fiscal year 2017
Original ANDA	60 percent in 15 months	75 percent in 15 months	90 percent in 10 months.
Tier 1 first major amendment	60 percent in 10 months	75 percent in 10 months	190 percent in 10 months.
Tier 1 minor amendments (1st–3d)	60 percent in 3 months*	75 percent in 3 months*	190 percent in 3 months*.
Tier 1 minor amendments (4th–5th).	60 percent in 6 months*	75 percent in 6 months*	90 percent in 6 months*.
Tier 2 amendment	60 percent in 12 months	75 percent in 12 months	90 percent in 12 months.
Prior approval supplements	60 percent in 6 months*	75 percent in 6 months*	90 percent in 6 months*.
ANDA teleconference requests	Close-out 200	Close-out 250	Close-out 300.
Controlled correspondences	60 percent in 4 months*	70 percent in 2 months*	90 percent in 2 months.

---

[1] http://www.fda.gov/downloads/ForIndustry/UserFees/GenericDrugUserFees/UCM282505.pdf.

[2] A prior approval supplement is a post approval change requiring supplemental submission and approval prior to distribution of the product made using the change.

[3] Tentative approval applies if a generic drug product is otherwise ready for approval before the expiration of any patents or exclusivities accorded to the *reference listed drug* product. In such instances, FDA issues a tentative approval letter to the applicant. FDA delays final approval of the generic drug product until all patent or exclusivity issues have been resolved. A tentative approval does not allow the applicant to market the generic drug product.

[4] A "refuse-to-receive" decision indicates that FDA determined that an ANDA is not sufficiently complete to permit a substantive review.

Chart 4. Major GDUFA Performance Goals**—Continued

Goals	Fiscal year 2015	Fiscal year 2016	Fiscal year 2017
ANDA, amendment and PAS in backlog on Oct 1, 2012.	Act on 90 percent by end of fiscal year 2017.		

*10 months if inspection required.

**Performance goals in the chart means FDA should take an action on a certain percent of applications, etc. within the timeframes listed; it does not mean FDA should approve applications, etc. within such timeframes.

To date, FDA has met or exceeded all performance goals outlined in the GDUFA Commitment Letter.

ACTIONS ON PRE-GDUFA ("BACKLOG") APPLICATIONS

A major commitment of GDUFA was to take a "first action" on 90 percent of the "backlog" applications, defined as pre-GDUFA applications pending before the Agency on October 1, 2012, by the end of fiscal year 2017. As of October 1, 2012, the backlog included 2,866 ANDAs and 1,873 PASs. As Chart 5 indicates, to date, FDA has completed first actions on 84 percent of ANDAs and 88 percent of PASs. And so, FDA is well ahead of schedule in achieving the GDUFA goal to significantly reduce the backlog, and our ultimate goal of eliminating it.

Chart 5. Percentage of Backlog Applications with First Action

First Actions 10/1/2012 to 12/31/2015

Actions	ANDAs	PAS
Number with First Action**	2,414	1,666
Percentage Complete	**84 percent**	**88 percent**
Approval	609	959
Tentative Approval	151	4
Complete Response with Inspection*	1,384	465
Refuse to Receive	69	2
Withdrawn Applications	201	236

*Complete Response with an Inspection is a written FDA communication to an applicant usually describing all of the deficiencies that the agency has identified in an application that must be satisfactorily addressed before it can be approved.

**Numbers are based on current data and will be further scrubbed for formal reporting purposes.

Some of these backlog applications had been pending or in review for a long time prior to GDUFA. At this point in time, as FDA acts on one of the outstanding backlog applications, the "time to approval" of such application will be recorded as, at minimum, 40 months (i.e., we now are 3 years and 4 months (40 months) into GDUFA implementation). This helps to explain the often-quoted 42 month approval time, which does not apply to post-GDUFA applications as explained below.

Moreover, the filing backlog for ANDAs has been eliminated. "Filing" is where we evaluate if a drug sponsor's submitted application is sufficiently complete to permit FDA's substantive review. In August 2014, we had a filing backlog of over 1,100 applications. Now that backlog is gone.

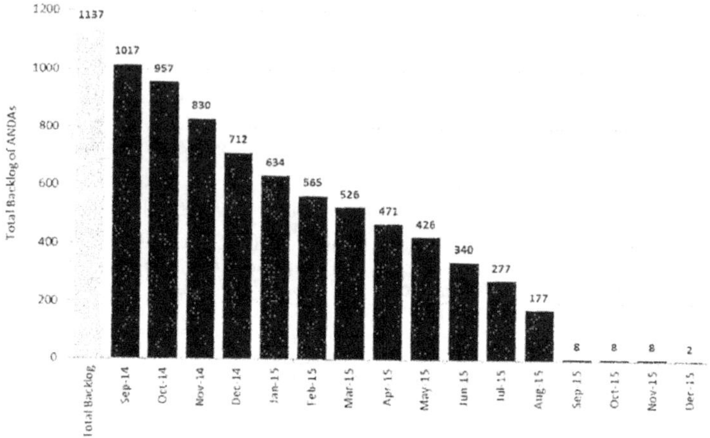

Chart 6. ANDA Filing Backlog

ACTIONS ON POST-GDUFA ORIGINAL APPLICATIONS [5]

In addition to the pre-GDUFA backlog applications, nearly 2,500 applications were submitted in fiscal year 2013 and fiscal year 2014 after GDUFA had commenced. Per the GDUFA Commitment Letter, these fiscal year 2013 and fiscal year 2014 applications have *no* GDUFA goal dates. Notwithstanding this, FDA assigned internal goals, called "Target Action Dates" (TADs), to both the pre-GDUFA backlog applications and to the fiscal year 2013 and fiscal year 2014 applications and has been aggressively reviewing them.

Under the GDUFA Commitment Letter, applications submitted in fiscal year 2015 have a 15 month "first-action" goal date. Goal dates represent a paradigm shift. They substantially improve the speed and predictability of review. So, any concerns about delayed competition in the generic space pertain to prior years, when our backlog was accumulating, and not to applications with GDUFA goal dates.

Importantly, if the ANDA submission is a potential "first generic" or could mitigate a drug shortage, its review is expedited. The performance goals for those generic applications submitted in the first few months of fiscal year 2015 are just coming due. We are on track to meet or exceed our obligations under the GDUFA Commitment Letter relative to these applications and already have approved or otherwise acted on some applications submitted in fiscal year 2015.

Applications submitted in fiscal year 2016 also have a first-action goal date of 15 months, with the Agency committed to reviewing a greater percentage of generic applications within the timeframe specified.

The cumulative result of all this effort is a huge increase in the productivity of the generics program. As Chart 7 indicates, we ended last year at a new monthly high of 99 approvals and tentative approvals in December.

---

[5] In this context, "Original Applications" refer to the first ANDA submitted, as opposed to a subsequent amendment or supplement to the ANDA.

Chart 7. Approvals and Tentative Approvals

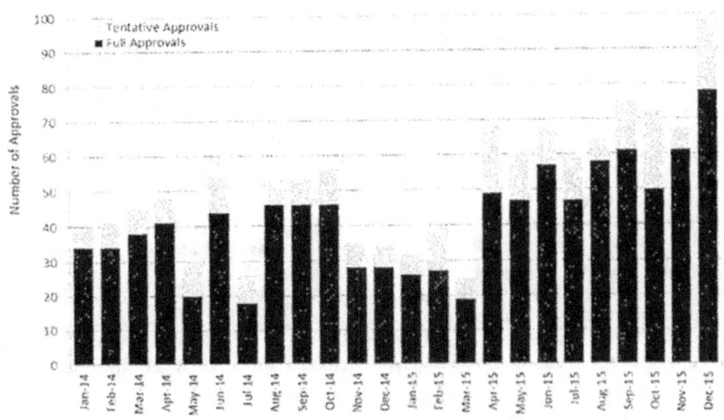

Of course, a major goal of GDUFA is timely approval of affordable, high-quality generic drugs. FDA's success in implementing the Prescription Drug User Fee Amendments (PDUFA) program—the user fee program for new drugs begun in 1992—provided the Agency with valuable experience that enabled us to rapidly build a modern generic drug review process once sufficient resources were made available through user fees. FDA is now on track to achieve the throughput needed, with sustained levels of record or near-record approvals in the third and fourth quarter of 2015.

PRIORITIZATION OF FIRST GENERICS APPLICATIONS

We recognize that certain types of applications merit priority attention based on their public health significance.

For example, we consider "first generics" to be public health priorities, as they can lead to increased patient access. First generics are just what they sound like—the first generic versions of a drug to enter the market. Under GDUFA, beginning in fiscal year 2015, each of these first generic submissions automatically receives a 15 month goal date. FDA has worked hard to provide an even faster review for potential first generics. Because they are public health priorities, we expedite their review, like an express lane at the supermarket.

Thanks to GDUFA, we made substantial first generic program improvements. We opened a docket to solicit technical input; issued a public-facing, transparent prioritization policy;[6] formed a team to expedite the review of first generics; trained review staff; and enhanced our computer systems to streamline the process.

Potential first generics are approximately 15 percent of our overall workload. All of these have been going in the "express lane." Over the past 3 years we have approved hundreds of first generics for over 200 new drug products. Significant first generic approvals for 2015, and the indications (abbreviated) for which these products were approved, are listed on the next page.

Significant First Generic Approvals for 2015

Brand (generic name)	Indications (abbreviated)
Abilify® (aripiprazole)	Schizophrenia, Bipolar Disorder.
Fusilev® (levoleucovorin)	Supports cancer treatment.
Enablex® (darifenacin)	Overactive bladder.
Lotronex® (alosetron)	Irritable bowel syndrome.
Zyvox® (linezolid)	Pneumonia, serious infections.
Tygacil® (tigecycline)	Pneumonia, serious infections.
Vagifem® (estradiol)	Menopause.
Integrelin® (eptifibatide)	Heart attack.

---

6 http://www.fda.gov/downloads/AboutFDA/CentersOffices/OfficeofMedicalProductsandTobacco/CDER/ManualofPoliciesProcedures/UCM407849.pdf.

Significant First Generic Approvals for 2015—Continued

Brand (generic name)	Indications (abbreviated)
Xenazine® (tetrabenazine)	Huntington's Disease.

PROGRESS ON ADDITIONAL IMPORTANT GDUFA GOALS

In addition to reducing the backlog, acting on post-GDUFA applications, and approving first generics, FDA is also achieving other important GDUFA goals.

One goal addressed risk-based inspection parity for foreign and domestic facilities. Before 2012, the law required us to inspect domestic facilities at a 2-year interval, but was silent on frequency for foreign establishments, regardless of their relative risk. GDUFA directs us to target inspections globally on the basis of risk. We are on track to achieve the goal of risk-based inspection parity between foreign and domestic facilities by the end of fiscal year 2017.

GDUFA also established goals for our review of PASs. PASs are important because they enable flexibility and improvements for generic drug manufacturing. To date, we have substantially exceeded GDUFA PAS goal of 60 percent reviewed within 6 months if an inspection is not required and 10 months if an inspection is required.

Chart 8. Exceeding Prior Approval Supplements (PAS) Review Goals*

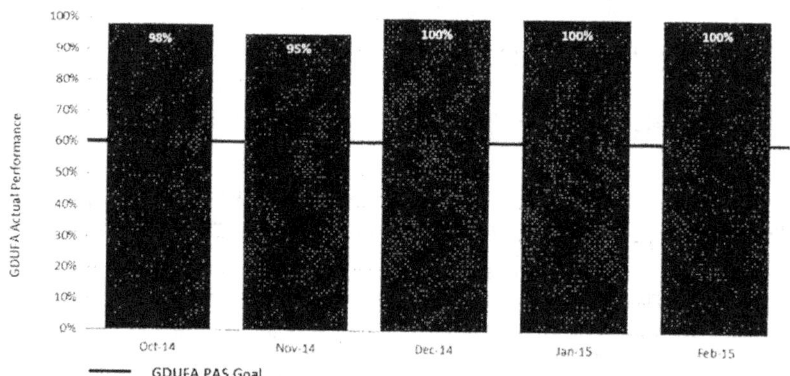

*Goal dates provided through February 2015, as those are the goal dates that have actually accrued. The cohort data is not mature enough to report on whole year data

There are also GDUFA goals for responding to controlled correspondence. Controlled correspondences are product development questions that FDA answers to help companies develop applications. The GDUFA goal for fiscal year 2015 was to respond to 70 percent within 4 months of submission. As noted in Chart 9, we substantially exceeded our commitments in this area.

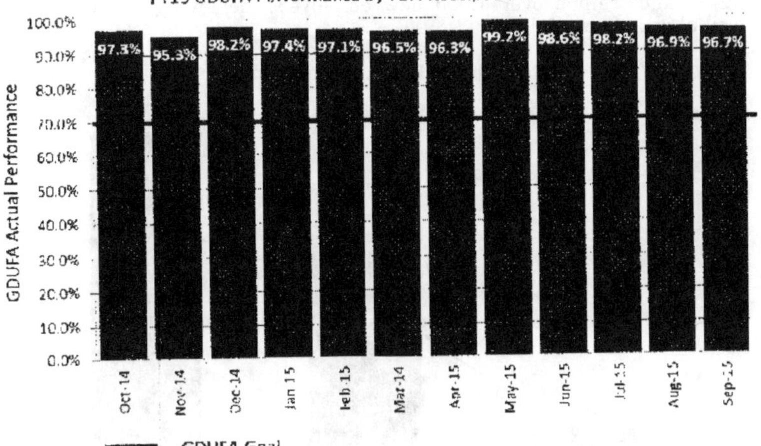

We also had a significant backlog of controlled correspondence from before goal dates started. We have eliminated that backlog.

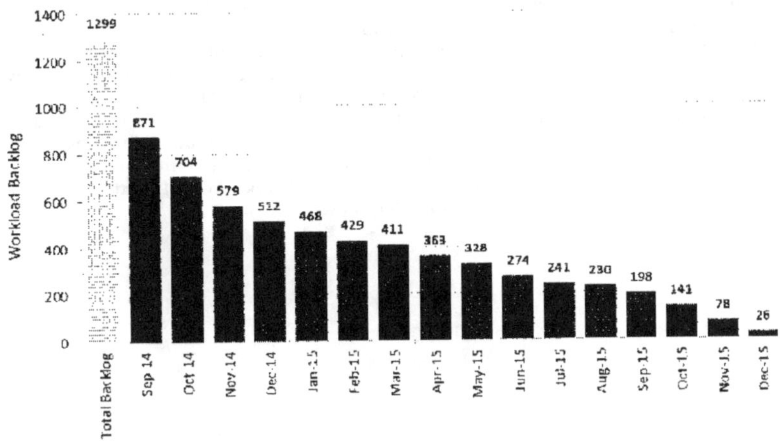

HOW DID FDA ACHIEVE THESE RESULTS?

Deep, foundational restructuring.

We achieved these results by building a modern generic drug program.

This involved major reorganizations. We reorganized the Office of Generic Drugs and elevated it to "Super-Office" status, on par with the Office of New Drugs. We established a new Office of Pharmaceutical Quality[7] to integrate the quality components of the review.

---

[7] http://www.fda.gov/AboutFDA/CentersOffices/OfficeofMedicalProductsandTobacco/CDER/ucm418347.htm.

We developed an integrated informatics platform to support the generic drug review process. It is a significant improvement over our fragmented, legacy systems, and has enhanced our productivity.

We hired and trained over 1,000 new employees, achieving our GDUFA hiring goals well ahead of schedule.

Chart 11. GDUFA Hiring Progress

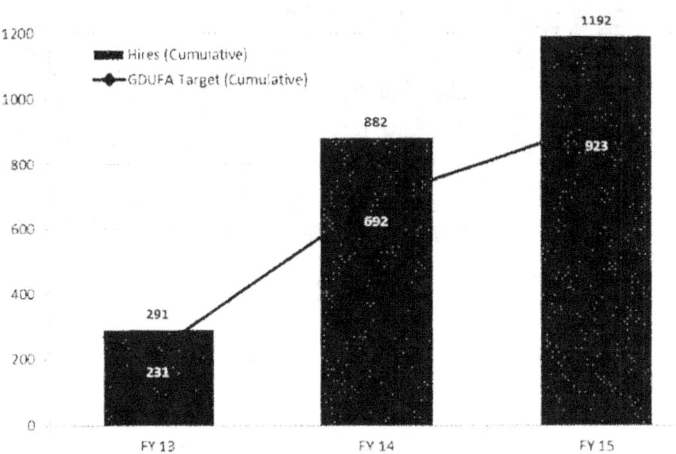

Flexible Approach: Communications and Transparency

We also took a flexible approach to managing the program in ways that benefit generic drug sponsors and, ultimately, patients.

One example of fine-tuning the process to speed approvals is the "Information Request" process. As originally agreed during the GDUFA negotiations, FDA was to package all deficiencies found in the review of an application and provide them to the applicant in a complete response letter. But that turned out not to be a helpful approach and industry asked us to send them information concerning individual deficiencies on a rolling basis, instead of consolidating them all into one package. This would help industry correct deficiencies in "real time." We agreed. In fiscal year 2015, we issued over 4,700 Information Requests.

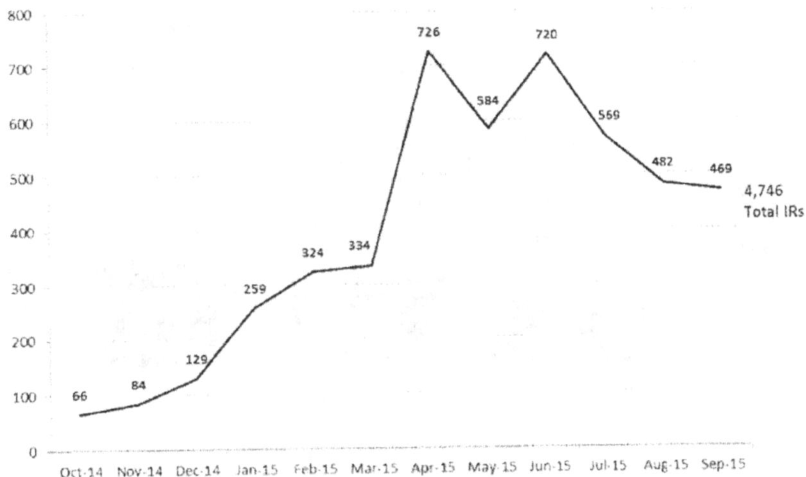

At industry's request, we communicated "Target Action Dates" (TADs). As previously described, TADs are our internal deadlines for action on all applications without goal dates. Although GDUFA did not require the Agency to develop TADs or communicate them to industry, we understand that they help companies plan product launches, spurring timely access to generics.

We also reacted to much larger than expected ANDA submission volume. As the GDUFA Commitment Letter stated, GDUFA review goals and planning were based on the assumption that the Agency would receive approximately 750 ANDAs per year. We budgeted and planned with this projection in mind. However, in fiscal years 2012, 2013 and 2014, we received over 1,000, nearly 1,000, and nearly 1,500 applications, respectively. We had to modify our planning and execution accordingly.

Chart 13. Projected vs. Actual ANDA Receipts

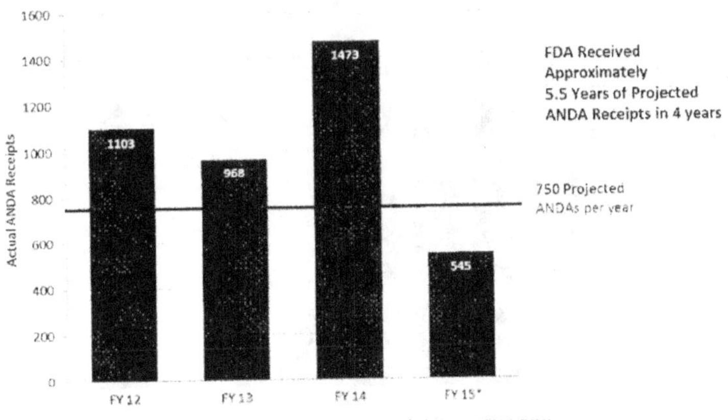

In addition, we increased our output of product-specific guidances. These guidances clarify our expectations concerning specific products so industry can develop and obtain approval of generic versions of branded drugs more quickly.

Chart 14. Product-Specific ANDA Guidances

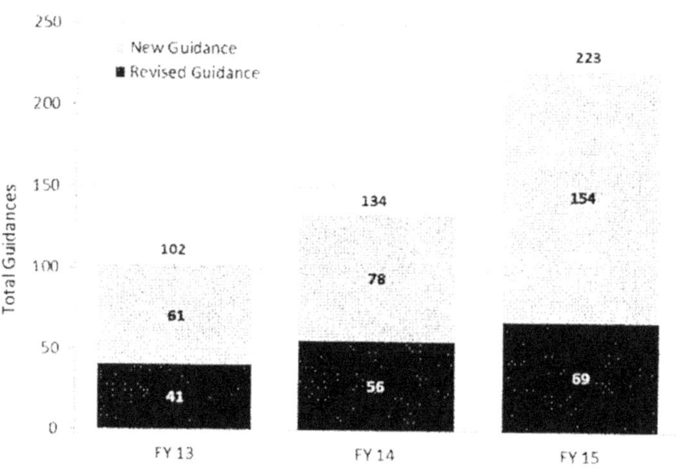

ONGOING CHALLENGES

We do have some ongoing challenges. The first relates to submission quality. Historically, it has taken on average about 4 review cycles to approve an ANDA as a result of deficiencies by generic drug sponsors in submitting complete and quality applications (see Chart 15). This has resulted in the submission of numerous amendments to correct deficiencies in the original ANDAs and comprises a huge amount of re-work for FDA and industry alike. Currently, for example, nearly 900 applications are back with industry awaiting resubmission to correct deficiencies in the original applications. New filing policies will help, but more work by both the Agency and industry will be necessary to have the filings be "right the first time."

Chart 15. Review Cycles for ANDAs
2009 through July 2014

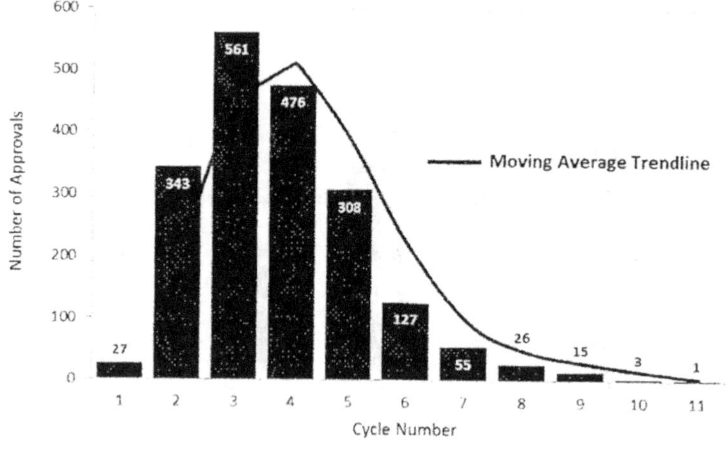

As noted in the public minutes[8] published as part of the GDUFA II negotiations now underway, FDA and industry are discussing a pre-ANDA process by which FDA and industry would address approval challenges for particular drugs prior to ANDA submissions, which could make a big difference in the completeness and quality of applications.

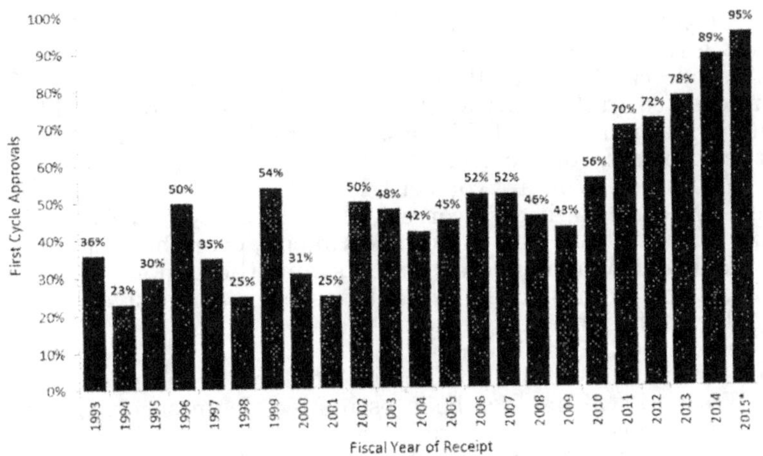

Chart 16. First Cycle Approval Rate Under PDUFA

CDER NME NDAs/BLAs[†]

First Action Approval Rate

Improvement may take some time. As Chart 16 shows, in the first few years of the PDUFA program, the first cycle approval rate dropped as low as 23 percent. Now it is 95 percent. Achieving this was the result of many years of work on standards and expectations.

Second, there is a need for more research in the generics space. Some drugs lack generic competition because there is no convincing bioequivalence test method available. In these instances, a more extensive clinical study is needed to show equivalence of a generic to a brand name drug. Similarly, methods for showing chemical sameness for certain complex drugs are not available. GDUFA provided funding for research efforts to work out these problems. So far, GDUFA has funded $34.9 million in research programs that will open up previously blocked pathways. However, scientific research takes time, and results will need to be translated into guidance for industry.

Third, shared system Risk Evaluation and Mitigation Strategies—or REMS—pose challenges. REMS are used to ensure that the benefits of drugs outweigh their risks. The statutory requirement that REMS programs that include elements to assure safe use (ETASU) be implemented through a "single shared system" relies on brand and generic companies to agree on such a system before generic drugs may come to market. This is challenging to implement and frequently results in blocking generic competition. We would welcome the opportunity to discuss possible solutions to this problem with you.

Fourth, to better assure quality in an increasingly globalized industry, FDA is undertaking major changes in quality regulation. CDER's Office of Pharmaceutical Quality, FDA's Program Alignment Group[9] and the International Council for Harmonisation[10] are all driving major changes, and FDA is pursuing mutual reliance discussions with the European Union. As a result of this work and collaborative effort, the public can be assured that FDA will hold generic products to the same quality standards as brand drugs, no matter where they are manufactured or tested.

---

[8] http://www.fda.gov/ForIndustry/UserFees/GenericDrugUserFees/ucm256662.htm.

[9] http://www.fda.gov/AboutFDA/CentersOffices/ucm392733.htm.

[10] http://www.ich.org/home.html.

CONCLUSION

I am extremely proud of what the FDA staff has accomplished in implementing GDUFA. Getting to where we are today has taken an enormous amount of work and above-and-beyond dedication by many people over the past 3 years. I have no doubt that we will exceed the goals initially established for this program.

GDUFA II discussions between the Agency and Industry are underway and constructive. We are excited and positive about the opportunity to make significant program improvements.

Thank you for the opportunity to describe what we've accomplished over the past 3 years. I look forward to your questions.

The CHAIRMAN. Thank you, Dr. Woodcock. We will now begin a series of a round of 5-minute questions.

Dr. Woodcock, I think all of us on the panel, maybe every Senator interested in drug prices that are as low as is reasonable, the statutory mission of the FDA is safe and effective drugs; it is not to set drug prices. Am I correct?

Dr. WOODCOCK. You are correct.

The CHAIRMAN. Is it also correct, though, that one of the effects of—and that you just said in your testimony, over the last 30 years with the Hatch-Waxman amendments and the generic movement that has gone from 0 to 88 percent has been a massive reduction or avoidance of higher drug prices.

Dr. WOODCOCK. That is correct.

The CHAIRMAN. And did you say $1.7 trillion in savings?

Dr. WOODCOCK. That has been estimated. I am sorry. One point seven trillion has been estimated.

The CHAIRMAN. One point seven trillion dollars. And it would make sense, then, that we should focus our attention on ways to continue to make generic drugs available to as many people as possible. Two ways we have sought to do that in the committee are to avoid unnecessary regulatory burdens and to make sure we have a competitive marketplace where prices are low.

I want to ask you, and you invited this really, about the backlog. Thirty years ago, the hope was that generic approvals could be 180 days. There was a backlog of 4,700 applications waiting to be reviewed, I guess, in 2012 if I am not mistaken. Then there have been a lot more applications since then. You described those. The median approval for a time to get review of a generic drug was 30 months 4 years ago. Today, the approval time seems to be higher, 48 months, and you are approving about the same number of new drugs. Yet over that period of time you have collected $1 billion and hired 1,000 new people. What can we do about the backlog and the approval time? Help us understand what the facts are.

Dr. WOODCOCK. Well, let me walk you through this. It is a little complicated. The backlog applications that were sitting there in 2012 when we put the program in place, have been there for 40 months. We have approved a lot of them. We have taken action on 82 percent of these, all right, some type of action. We have gone back to the manufacturer, they have withdrawn some, and so forth, right? But they have been there since 2012, so even if we approved all of them tomorrow, their approval time would be 40 months because that was 40 months ago. And the longer it takes, just like the rest of us, they are not getting any younger. So those applications that were sitting there in 2012 are going to, at minimum, have total time to approval of 40 months because they started 40 months ago.

The ones that we are getting in now have a due date for a complete response of 15 months. We have already approved some in the previous cohort last year that had 15-month timeframe. We approved a drug in 9 months on the first——

The CHAIRMAN. So you are saying the new applications have a different median time?

Dr. WOODCOCK. They do. They were the first ones that had goals. None of these others, the 2012 pending and then the first 2 years of the program had no goals assigned to them.

The CHAIRMAN. What about the number of approvals today as compared with a few years ago?

Dr. WOODCOCK. If you look at the chart in my testimony, you will see that in the first 2 years of GDUFA we did not jump up approvals. It was pretty much up and down. In April of last year, approvals went up, and they have stayed up. And as I said, last month, we approved or TA'ed 99 generic drugs.

So we are on a path to get these efficiently out the door now. We had to build the program. We had to get this IT system. We had to hire and train these people.

The CHAIRMAN. If I may have one more question, and I do not want to go over my time, I want to make sure that you are making the distinction between what a guidance requires and a regulation requires. I know the Office of Management and Budget is interested in that. And I have heard some concerns about one proposed guidance on quality for generic manufacturers that would impose new obligations to submit reports. Are you making a distinction between guidances which do not have the rule of law and regulations which may have the rule of law but do require a certain amount of public comment?

Dr. WOODCOCK. We certainly do. As part of implementing this program, we have put a policy office in the Office of Generic Drugs and established a new policy office in the Office of Pharmaceutical Quality, which does the quality regulation. And both of those offices, part of their function, their staff, partly by lawyers, is to make sure we follow good guidance practices and follow the appropriate practices for regulations.

The CHAIRMAN. Thank you very much, Dr. Woodcock.

Senator Murray.

Senator MURRAY. Dr. Woodcock, as I mentioned in my opening statement, Hatch-Waxman has been an incredible success and has provided patients and families with access to high-quality, lower-cost drugs. And building on that success, this committee's bipartisan work to pass the Generic Drug User Fee Amendments provided FDA with the resources to tackle existing backlog.

Some are now saying that the backlog of generic applications remaining at FDA is part of the reason patients and families are experiencing high drug costs. How do you respond to those claims?

Dr. WOODCOCK. The high drug costs are driven by multiple factors, but one might be lack of competition. So is there a generic competitor for the innovator product? And those we call the first generic, the first generic to get on the market, which begins to lower the price. We have looked at all these backlogs, and there is nothing in that backlog that would be a first generic potentially. Even if it is one or two applications, either of those could be the first generic that we have not looked at.

We cannot approve applications even as a first generic if they do not meet our standards, if they are substandard in some way or if they are incomplete. So we may not always approve every application that comes before us that is a first generic, but we expedite those products.

Senator MURRAY. The first generic?

Dr. WOODCOCK. We absolutely do. And they get a fast track through the process, and we make sure we pay attention to those. I can assure you that in that backlog that was sitting there in 2012 and that we are working on now that we have largely worked on, that there is nothing that has not been looked at and given attention and certainly that would provide a first generic.

Senator MURRAY. When FDA does approve those potential first generic applications, do companies usually market those generic drugs right away?

Dr. WOODCOCK. No, we do not understand the behavior of companies and of course sometimes it's difficult to ascertain what they are doing in the market, as Senator Collins' hearing with the Aging Committee demonstrated. But we have noticed that, often, companies will not market a product sometimes for a significant amount of time after they have received an approval for first generic.

Senator MURRAY. OK. Yesterday, the HHS assistant secretary for planning and evaluation came out with the report about the generic drug market, concluding that generic drug prices are not the primary driver of the high drug cost facing many patients and families across the country. The report found that the generic drug market as a whole is quite competitive, although some segments have experienced large price increases. What type of competition exists for innovator drugs currently on the market? What does that mean for patients?

Dr. WOODCOCK. With your permission, I would like to bring up a slide if I could. This one I think would be good.

[Slide.]

It is just a simple bar chart. It shows the 99 on the left is the number of innovator drugs that only have one generic competitor. There are 66 that have two generic competitors, and all the rest have 3 to 10 generic competitors, which has been shown to really bring the price down when there is that much competition in the market.

In addition—could I have the pie chart?

[Slide.]

If you look at this pie chart, it is a picture of all the drugs that would be out there. If you look at the silver slice, that is innovator drugs that could have a generic competitor but do not. And many of those are orphans or very small market drugs.

Senator MURRAY. OK.

Dr. WOODCOCK. There is a remaining group of products. It is small, but that is where we see a lot of the action as far as price changes when generic competition is possible.

Senator MURRAY. OK. I am told that it typically takes three approved generics before we see real pricing competition kick in and prices go down. How many innovator drugs have reached the level of having three generic competitors? Is that your number there——

Dr. WOODCOCK. Yes.

Senator MURRAY [continuing]. The six——

Dr. WOODCOCK. You can see, the vast majority have large enough sales, I imagine, that multiple competitors get in the market.

Senator MURRAY. And that is what drives the price?

Dr. WOODCOCK. Yes.

Senator MURRAY. OK. You mentioned how the FDA generics program is on its way to being a real success story because of the resources Congress provided. I wanted to just ask you, can you describe the current status of FDA's generics workload?

Dr. WOODCOCK. Yes. Could I have another chart?

[Slide.]

This chart shows the entire workload at almost the current time. At the top, the number—this is too complicated, I am afraid, but at the top, the 6,218 is all the applications we have had to deal with since the program started. The bottom number, 600, those are the ones that have not entered review yet. So that is only 10 percent that have not entered review. And some of those were submitted very recently.

Twenty-four hundred were in the stage of back and forth with companies. So we are going back and forth. We are trying not to have these multiple cycles like we had in the past but get the issues resolved during the review process and try to get to a first-cycle approval.

Senator MURRAY. So when people say backlog, it is not like the drug is sitting there and nothing is happening to it. It is part of the backlog even if it has been withdrawn by the company or you are going back and forth with the company?

Dr. WOODCOCK. Well, this is simply the overall workload——

Senator MURRAY. Yes.

Dr. WOODCOCK [continuing]. And the backlog was something that existed——

Senator MURRAY. Prior?

Dr. WOODCOCK [continuing]. In 2012, right. In the future, we are not going to have any backlogs. We are going to have—if we get 1,000 drugs submitted a year, applications, we are going to have a bunch in process. They will not be in backlog because they will have goal dates. They will simply be moving down the process.

But because we have a lot of them that do not have goal dates now, although we have assigned them action dates, this is a better description of——

Senator MURRAY. Got you.

Dr. WOODCOCK [continuing]. Where they all are, I think, even though it is overly complicated. So you see that almost 600 have been withdrawn by the firms, and we have approved 1,500, tentatively approved 268. And we are working on these 2,400 so that is 4,000 that have either been approved, tentatively approved, or we are talking to the companies.

Senator MURRAY. All right. OK. Thank you very much.

Dr. WOODCOCK. Thank you.

The CHAIRMAN. Thank you, Senator Murray.

Next, Senator Collins and Casey, then Cassidy, then Franken.

Senator Collins.

STATEMENT OF SENATOR COLLINS

Senator COLLINS. Thank you, Mr. Chairman.

Dr. Woodcock, first, let me thank you for your many years of public service and all that you are doing to expedite generic drug applications in order to make prescription drugs more affordable for consumers.

I know that you are familiar with the investigation the Aging Committee is doing into the sudden very aggressive price spikes that some companies have implemented on drugs that have been on the market for literally decades. One, Daraprim, is 63 years old, and yet there has been a 5,000 percent increase in its price by a company that invested not one dime into the research and development that led to this drug.

So I am concerned that our current regulatory structure does not take into account situations where there is essentially a market failure. Because the population of patients may be small, there is not generic application, whether it is pending or not. It just has not happened.

I know that the FDA currently provides an express lane review for certain generic drug applications, including first generics and those that would help solve medical drug shortages. Could you give us some idea of what the timeline is for the expedited review for drugs for the first generics or those that are in the medical shortages category?

Dr. WOODCOCK. They get to the front of the queue. And of course with so many applications coming through, we can expedite different things. We have to treat them fairly. All would get expedited in the same way. So they get extra attention. They get moved to the review queue front, so they get reviewed first, and people shepherd them through. But if they are substandard in any way, under our new process, of course, we will call the manufacturer and try to get that application repaired. But say we go inspect the facility and it is substandard, we are still not going to approve that drug. But we do move them along as fast as possible.

For the cohort that comes in after September of this year, there is going to be a 10-month review clock. That is the goal. That is for all generic drugs. So somebody who submits a generic drug October 1 of this year can expect a 10-month review. And if we are successful, they will get an approval at the end, not a lot of questions about their application.

That is pretty expedited as it is, especially since they have facilities often in China and India and different places around the country may have to check.

Senator COLLINS. Let me ask you about a situation with two of the drugs that we are looking at the Aging Committee's investigation: Isuprel and Nitropress. And these two drugs once had FDA-approved generic competitors, but over time, those competitors left the market and now there is only one manufacturer left. So if a new manufacturer were to come in now, would that application be expedited?

Dr. WOODCOCK. That is a good question and we will take it back and try to figure out what our policy should be on that because it would be akin to a first generic, although technically not a first generic.

Senator COLLINS. That is why I ask it.

Dr. WOODCOCK. Part of our problem is knowing who has marketed when. These people sort of come in and out of the market. If they do not withdraw their applications, it is hard for us to say whether they are marketing unless we get notified of a shortage, in which case, it becomes clear.

Senator COLLINS. The other related issue that I would ask you to work with us on as we try to come up with solutions to these market failures is figuring out what the length of time for an expedited approval should be that would discourage the company from buying up a decades-old drug and increasing the cost of it? If it is a short enough time, it is not going to be worth the amount of money that the manufacturer—well, they are not manufacturers; they are more like what I would call hedge fund pharmaceutical companies—would pay to get the rights to that drug.

So one of the ideas that I would like to work with you on is whether there is a way to take away the incentive by having this expedited approval that would encourage a generic to come in and discourage the company from buying up the decades-old drug thinking it is going to have a monopoly long enough to make a great deal of money.

Dr. WOODCOCK. We would be happy to work with you. We also have to consider there is development work that a company has to do. They cannot just turn a switch and start manufacturing a drug tomorrow. So there is that time that has to go in as well.

Senator COLLINS. What we are finding is that a lot of these companies are not doing the manufacturing, and so it is a very new and interesting business model, and I am convinced that it is one that is really negative for patients, providers, hospitals, and for Federal and State health care programs.

Dr. WOODCOCK. Mr. Chairman, may I just make an editorial comment?

The CHAIRMAN. Yes.

Dr. WOODCOCK. Thank you. We have talked to some Members in the House and some of you all about advanced manufacturing and our efforts on this. Why we like advanced manufacturing, we are trying to push it with the industry is that allows them really to turn very quickly and really ramp up very fast——

The CHAIRMAN. Do you want to define advanced manufacturing, what you mean by that?

Dr. WOODCOCK. Certainly. Potato chips and M&Ms and all sorts of foods in this country and fine chemicals are made in continuous manufacturing lines that are computer-controlled, automobiles, even with robots. Pharmaceuticals are not made that way. They are made almost like cooking would be familiar or pharmacy compounding, steps. And we are really trying to push to move to modernized computer-controlled continuous manufacturing. It is much more efficient and effective, but of course there——

The CHAIRMAN. Are you talking like 3-D printing?

Dr. WOODCOCK. This year, we approved a 3-D printed product, the first one this year. So also that is one of the aspects that enables doing things like that, yes. That is an aspect I think that we really should explore to provide agility into the system.

Thank you.

Senator COLLINS. Thank you, Mr. Chairman. I apologize for going over my time.

The CHAIRMAN. No, no, thank you and thank you, Dr. Woodcock, for that.

Senator Collins, we know that in the Committee on Aging, you and Senator McCaskill have done a lot of work on this subject. We know also you do not have legislative authority, so we welcome the work product from your committee over here as we work on our legislation.

Senator COLLINS. Thank you.

The CHAIRMAN. Senator Casey.

Senator Franken.

STATEMENT OF SENATOR FRANKEN

Senator FRANKEN. Thank you. I appreciate Senator Collins' questions.

And part of your answer, it seemed to suggest that the data that you have on the market is not totally complete.

Dr. WOODCOCK. That is correct.

Senator FRANKEN. And is there anything you can do—is that an aspiration of yours to make that data more complete?

Dr. WOODCOCK. It is very difficult to figure these things out because as——

Senator FRANKEN. Who would do that, do you think?

Dr. WOODCOCK. I believe in Senator Collins' hearing they talked about the contracts and the rebates and all the different things in the U.S. distribution chain that nobody really knows the answer to. And the insurers, I think, would really like to know how these drugs are moving and what is actually being paid for them at different steps. But they do not know, and that is what I took from the testimony.

Senator FRANKEN. OK.

Dr. WOODCOCK. We can find out sort of ex post facto by looking at what has been dispensed at the end of the day and putting the picture together, but it is very difficult to say who is—because they shift——

Senator FRANKEN. To try and figure that out would inform what you are taking up to approve because you want to make the market more efficient.

I want to ask you about an article in the Wall Street Journal this week, and I am sure you have read it. It was by the CEO of a drug compounding company, and he suggested that basically he pointed to a drug that his company did. And we took up compounding in this committee, and a number of us, including the Chairman and Senator Roberts. But he was basically saying that he did successfully compound a drug, a generic that had been one of these drugs that they exploded the price on, and he got to market by compounding this.

We saw the risks associated with compounding, but then we also gave the FDA authority to regulate compounding. You read this piece. Do you think that there are risks to this? What is the upside and what are the risks?

Dr. WOODCOCK. I believe there are very great risks. The Congress established outsourcing facilities as part of the reestablishment of compounding several years ago, but those are for sterile injectables. The tablets could be compounded by any compounding facility under what was being proposed. And in the last 2 months, we have dealt with two outbreaks. One was vitamins where they compounded vitamins, and way excessive vitamins were put into the tablet. People were hospitalized with kidney failure.

The second one——

Senator FRANKEN. Are vitamins considered supplements which you do not——

Dr. WOODCOCK. No, we regulated those and we intervened. We were able to track the people down. The second one was a hormone. It was 1,000 times more potent than it was supposed to be.

Senator FRANKEN. A thousand times? OK.

Dr. WOODCOCK. People ended up in the hospital very sick. And these were small outbreaks, so the pharmacy and us together were able to track these people down, the people who were still not in the hospital, and the drug was recalled. But a mass production of drugs such as to substitute for a generic or an innovator drug that is out there under non-controlled conditions—I know everybody talks about regulatory burdens, but what we ask them to do is make sure they do the right thing each time.

And this is what happened. They put in too much. They used the wrong source. They used an ultra-concentrated source, and they put people in the hospital. And if they had been making thousands of these tablets, they could have put thousands of people in the hospital. So that is what we face if alternative sources that do not have good manufacturing practices are going to go into mass production.

Senator FRANKEN. I am out of time but—so—yes, I am out of time. I am out of time.

[Laughter.]

The CHAIRMAN. But that is a very helpful question about two important pieces of legislation before this committee. That is a very, very interesting discussion.

Senator FRANKEN. Thank you.

The CHAIRMAN. Senator Cassidy.

STATEMENT OF SENATOR CASSIDY

Senator CASSIDY. Thank you, Dr. Woodcock. I echo Senator Collins' kind of compliments of your work, and also I always appreciate your straightforwardness.

A couple things, first—someone asked regarding backlog applications. You said at least 85 percent of those who are pre this legislation have had some action. That means 15 percent have not. I can imagine if you are one of that 15 percent you are just like, oh, my gosh.

Second, 85 percent have had some action. That action might have been to kick them back. So any comments on why is that 15 percent still kind of in purgatory and the 85 percent, ET cetera?

Dr. WOODCOCK. When we negotiated this agreement with industry, they were realistic that we were not going to be able to review 6,000 applications in 3 years and hire 1,000 people and rebuild our entire generic drug system and totally reorganize, all of which we have done.

So the goal was that we clear out 90 percent of the backlog applications by the end of the program, 5 years. That was the agreed-upon goal with industry, with no other intermediate goals. What we have done, we have already gotten back to them or worked on 82 percent of them.

Senator CASSIDY. Got you. I do not mean to interrupt; I just have a short time and I have so many questions.

Dr. WOODCOCK. OK.

Senator CASSIDY. Now, I am also told by industry—and I have learned to say "what I have been told" not "what I know"—that when you mentioned the incomplete or low-quality applications, sometimes they are low quality because in the interval between when it is submitted and when it is reviewed, the standards have changed. So it is now low quality not because it was low quality at the time of submission but because it is low quality at time of review. Are those applicants notified when standards change and the implications of that change in standard upon the quality of their initial application?

Dr. WOODCOCK. Absolutely, we try to do that. Our policy offices were issuing many more guidances. Those often are product-specific guidances. They are like a cookbook or recipe——

Senator CASSIDY. Then the followup question therefore implied is that you—because they tell me that this is not the case—that it has been made public, the guidance as to what is a good quality application?

Dr. WOODCOCK. We try. There are things such as we have received applications where they have cut-and-pasted portions from another application, totally the wrong application in there. It is hard to think of every single thing that people can do that is not right. But we do try to give guidance, and having our policy offices, we definitely aspire to putting out much more guidance and training on what is acceptable.

I have a slide in the——

Senator CASSIDY. Can I just move to something else?

Dr. WOODCOCK. Yes.

Senator CASSIDY. Because I will accept your explanation. And believe me, I will hear from them.

Next, following up on what Senator Collins has said, but also relating back to testimony you gave to the Energy and Commerce Committee a couple years ago when I was on that committee, one of the reasons for drug shortages is that there has been a concentration of drug manufacturers.

Dr. WOODCOCK. That is right.

Senator CASSIDY. If there is a quality problem with that one concentrated facility, then it ripples through. What I am told is that GDUFA actually has a facility fee, and therefore, if you only have one facility or if you contract out to a CMO, a contract manufacturing organization, that somehow you lower the facility fee. It would require us to change that. But because of this, we have had a concentration of manufacturing units. Is that a fair assessment?

Dr. WOODCOCK. I do not know whether that is a driven concentration or not. I think there are many factors, but that could have been one. We are certainly considering that in the discussions for the next GDUFA program.

Senator CASSIDY. Then we should consider that because it would require, say, a substitution of a product fee as opposed to a facility fee. Fair statement?

Dr. WOODCOCK. There are many different ways this could be. We are trying to make the fee structure as fair as possible and that the burden is shared appropriately among the people who benefit from the program.

Senator CASSIDY. Do you have a list of how many manufacturing units, if you will, there were or how many CMOs were active before GDUFA and what are the number of manufacturer facilities now post-GDUFA?

Dr. WOODCOCK. One of the innovations of GDUFA was self-identification. We have one 2012 where everybody had to put up their hand and say we are making a generic drug or we are making any active pharmaceutical ingredient. So we have it for those probably 3 years but not before. That was one of the defects in the past.

Senator CASSIDY. But still, if you had it when it started and you have it now, how many in 2012 and now, do you have that number?

Dr. WOODCOCK. We can get back to you on that. I do not have that.

Senator CASSIDY. And could you require the drug manufacturers to publish or say we are making these drugs and we are contracting out the CMOs for this, and have that as a real-time database? Because we need to know if we are concentrating manufacturers.

Dr. WOODCOCK. Right.

Senator CASSIDY. And if so—because you have told us that that is a major cause of drug shortages, and some of them are bad actors because you also told us that. Some have a lot of problems, some not. If that were made public, we would know how many there were and if they were good or bad actors. Is that possible for you to make that public or at least available to us?

Dr. WOODCOCK. I think that we could give you the overall numbers. We could try. But I think making the actual people public would probably require either regulation change or something Congress——

Senator CASSIDY. A statute for us to do?

Dr. WOODCOCK. Yes. There is registration and listing that is done now, but we have different problems with that, which we could get back to you on.

Senator CASSIDY. Thank you. I yield back. Thank you.

The CHAIRMAN. Thank you, Senator Cassidy.

Senator Warren.

STATEMENT OF SENATOR WARREN

Senator WARREN. Thank you, Mr. Chairman.

Everyone is here looking for ways to bring down the cost of drugs, both brand name and generic drugs, but we cannot do that if we do not correctly identify why the prices are so high. Some people want to blame the FDA for high prices saying that if the agency would approve generic drugs faster, then the drug pricing problem would go away.

So I just want to dig into that claim a little bit. Let us begin with generics competing with brand name drugs. According to an analysis by Harvard researchers, it takes an average of 12½ years for a brand name drug to face competition by generics. And no doubt if those brand name drugs had to compete with a generic drug, they would be cheaper. But the law is clear. The FDA cannot bring a generic drug to market while the brand name drug is still protected by any form of exclusivity or patents.

Dr. WOODCOCK. Patents.

Senator WARREN. Is that right?

Dr. WOODCOCK. That is correct.

Senator WARREN. OK. Then let us look at the time after generics are legally allowed on the market. How long does it take the FDA to approve a new application for a generic drug?

Dr. WOODCOCK. That is something that is in flux, but this year, it will take us 15 months on average to get back to the firm. If they have sent in a complete application, we can probably approve it.

Senator WARREN. That is for new applications?

Dr. WOODCOCK. Yes, the ones that are submitted this year.

Senator WARREN. And what commitment time are you looking at going forward?

Dr. WOODCOCK. In October of this year if you would submit a generic drug application, you could expect to get an answer back in 10 months.

Senator WARREN. In 10 months?

Dr. WOODCOCK. Correct.

Senator WARREN. So you are going from 15 months to 10 months. And you feel like you are on target at least getting the pieces in place that that looks like it is going to work?

Dr. WOODCOCK. That is doable, correct.

Senator WARREN. OK. Then I just want to measure that against the claim that the average time for FDA approval has increased. You talked about the backlog and the difficulty of dealing with applications that date back years, but the average time for new applications, is it going up or is it going down?

Dr. WOODCOCK. The new applications have not reached their sort of time to get approved yet, so we cannot really say. The goal has only kicked in last year, and that was a 15-month goal. But as I said, we already approved one at 9 months. We have approved a number of them that has been shorter than the 15-month goal.

Senator WARREN. That is right. And you are committing to a shorter time period?

Dr. WOODCOCK. We are committed to meeting the GDUFA goals for each cohort, that is correct.

Senator WARREN. All right. Then let me ask you one other question about this. When a company suddenly raises the price of a generic drug, obviously approval of a competing generic drug would probably bring the price back down. Dr. Woodcock, does the FDA expedite applications in situations when there has been a price spike?

Dr. WOODCOCK. No.

Senator WARREN. Why not?

Dr. WOODCOCK. We do not really know. We have to be fair. There are a lot of lawsuits around generic drugs and so forth. We have to be fair to all—we do not know what a price spike is. Does a pill cost 10 cents and now it costs 30 cents? Does it cost 10 cents and now it costs $875?

Senator WARREN. That one kind of sounds spiky to me.

[Laughter.]

Dr. WOODCOCK. Right. And we also do not, I think, have the expertise to determine. We are not economists or finance people. We are doctors and lawyers and scientists. So what we could——

Senator WARREN. Is it legally clear that you could do that? Could you use that as a criteria for deciding to expedite on a particular drug or is there some legal ambiguity about that?

Dr. WOODCOCK. There might be ambiguity, but certainly, if Congress directed us to prioritize certain drugs——

Senator WARREN. No, I am just asking about where you are right now.

Dr. WOODCOCK. OK. I do not know the answer to that specifically, but I imagine it might be possible if there were some bulletproof definition of what a price—what if you doubled your price from a dime to 20 cents?

Senator WARREN. This may be something we want to look at. I think that is helpful. But we will look at the proposals that are on the table today. Yes, Congress could make sure that the FDA has the funding and the personnel it needs. Yes, there is some room to improve generic drug approval processes as the new user fee program is fully implemented. Yes, there could be limited situations where the FDA might be able to expedite review of a generic drug to help lower prices. We are already heading toward 10-month approvals so that should help.

But let us not kid ourselves. Making those tweaks will not solve the drug pricing problem. The market for prescription drugs has little transparency, it has broken price elasticity, and it has very long legal monopolies. And, sure, we can make some changes, small changes to how the FDA approves generics, but real change will require us to face the fact that the market for prescription drugs is not working and rethink the overall structure of drug pricing.

Thank you, Dr. Woodcock. Thank you, Mr. Chairman.

The CHAIRMAN. Thank you, Senator Warren.

I have Senator Roberts, Senator Casey, Senator Burr, and Senator Murphy.

Senator Roberts.

STATEMENT OF SENATOR ROBERTS

Senator ROBERTS. Mr. Chairman, thank you. And thanks also to the Ranking Member for holding this hearing.

Everybody knows about the cost of prescription drugs. They continue to make headlines. And I truly appreciate Dr. Woodcock. You are an excellent witness, and thank you for your clarity and your comments.

In addition to new user fees in 2012, as has been said, the FDA has proposed a regulation in 2013 regarding generic labeling that according to one estimate could increase spending on generic drugs by billions of dollars.

In 2015, a proposed equality metrics program through draft guidance, draft guidance that would require manufacturers to collect new information and also to collect and report information from the CMOs, the generic drug manufacturers have raised significant concerns, I think to everybody here, regarding reporting complexity, the confidentiality of data, increased information technology spending, all of which would increase the burdens on the manufacturers and require significant efforts to resolve.

If these quality reports are to be required and obviously are necessary to ensure high-quality generic drugs, should this not be done through rulemaking? I would pause here and say this is the first time in my House or Senate career that I have ever proposed more rulemaking.

[Laughter.]

But rulemaking rather than a guidance——

Dr. WOODCOCK. Right.

Senator ROBERTS [continuing]. Where there is no responsibility to look at the impact on small business, and those who are involved cannot respond to comments, which to me seems to be very important.

Dr. WOODCOCK. Both of those, the regulation you mentioned first and then the draft guidance that we have issued some time ago on quality metrics, request for comments, a draft guidance is not actionable. It is simply a request for comments. So we did receive a great deal of comments on both of these, and we are in the time of digesting these comments. And we will take appropriate steps after we have gotten feedback.

But we have gotten a great deal of feedback on the quality metrics draft proposal both from the innovator industry and the generic industry, and actually, it is one of the few times where they appear to be united in their opinions. So we certainly are taking that into consideration in what we do next.

Senator ROBERTS. I appreciate that. I think most of the questions that I have here have already been asked by Members. The definition question that was raised I think by Senator Murray, in your testimony you highlighted the ongoing challenge of submission quality, and the question was have you made public, in guidance or otherwise, what the standard for good quality submissions is? When was that released, or have you released that?

Dr. WOODCOCK. It is a whole series of different guidances. For example, we issue product-specific guidance that tells you if you are going to copy this innovator product, here is how you should do your bioequivalence studies and so forth. And we have really ramped up our issuance of those because they are extremely helpful to industry.

Senator ROBERTS. How many folks do you have doing this?

Dr. WOODCOCK. The guidance development?

Senator ROBERTS. We are interested in 2015 and everybody left behind and those in the future. How many people do you have— about 1,000 people doing this? What is the answer?

Dr. WOODCOCK. There are approximately 1,000 people in the Office of Generic Drugs.

Senator ROBERTS. Right.

Dr. WOODCOCK. There are maybe 800, 900 people working on this in the Office of Pharmaceutical Quality that are inspectors. We added 70 new inspectors to do some of these foreign inspections. So the program is probably perhaps 3,000 people overall.

Senator ROBERTS. Three thousand people?

Dr. WOODCOCK. Yes.

Senator ROBERTS. I appreciate that. I have 30 seconds left, which I will yield back to Senator Franken, who needed more time.

Senator FRANKEN. It is going to take me about 25 seconds to recall——

[Laughter.]

Senator FRANKEN [continuing]. What it was, so I will yield my time.

The CHAIRMAN. Thank you for this outburst of bipartisanship.

Senator Casey.

STATEMENT OF SENATOR CASEY

Senator CASEY. Mr. Chairman, thank you very much.

Doctor, great to have you here, and thank you for your testimony and your service.

I wanted to focus on an area that I know you have spoken to, but I am not sure this specific question was asked about the so-called—we have to be careful with acronyms here—REMS, the risk evaluation mitigation strategy; and then the other acronym, the elements to assure safe use. The basic question I had was when you testified about some of the challenges that you have in implementing shared risk evaluation system, can you outline for us the challenges you face, and then if any—and I am assuming there are—what you propose as solutions?

Dr. WOODCOCK. When Congress, in the FDA Amendments Act, put in place the REMS, when they had to contemplate—and REMS is a risk evaluation and mitigation system for particularly risky drugs that is supposed to mitigate some of the risks. And we approve drugs with REMS if they are particularly risky.

When they go generic, the generics also need to have this risk system around them. And Congress, in order to decrease the burden on health care, said that if at all possible there be a single shared REMS amongst the innovator and the competitors.

To get competitors to work together so that the competitors can get a market share from the innovator has proven very challenging for the FDA to get that done, and that has delayed access.

In addition, the REMS program may restrict who gets the drug and that has been used as an excuse to not give the drug to the generics so they can compare it to their drug. All of these issues have caused barriers and delays in getting generics on the market.

More broadly, though, the companies on their own behalf have restricted programs that we do not really understand, but they are not related to REMS. We have had over 100 inquiries from generic companies who cannot get a hold of the innovator drug to compare their drug to. We have done everything we can to—we have written a letter saying that REMS does not require this, you can give it out for this purpose, and so forth, and we also refer these to FTC. But we still continue to get complaints from generic companies that they cannot get a hold of the drug to make the comparison they need to do.

Senator CASEY. I want to make sure I understand the problem you face. Why has it not worked in your judgment?

Dr. WOODCOCK. I think the innovator companies feel it is their duty to their stockholders to delay competition as long as possible. That is kind of—the citizen petitions we get and all sorts of things that attempt to delay generic competition. And this is yet another opportunity.

Senator CASEY. What would you hope that we would do, if anything?

Dr. WOODCOCK. The part of the REMS provision that requires a single shared system, as a practical matter, we have to try and try and try and try, and then finally, we declare defeat and we go ahead and let the generics have their own system that is separate but equal. If that provision were removed from a statute, then potentially, we could just go to that and it would not have a delay involved.

However, that will not fix the instance where the innovator company actually is not providing outside of REMS, so just have a way of not providing the drug to the generic company, and I think that would require discussions.

Senator CASEY. Thanks very much.

The CHAIRMAN. Thank you, Senator Casey.

Senator Hatch is next, but I think nobody will mind me saying it is not often that a U.S. Senator has a chance to introduce a significant piece of legislation and then 30 years later see it be as successful as this has been, taking the number of generic drugs prescribed from 0 to 88 percent of all the prescription drugs. So we welcome you to a hearing on your bill.

STATEMENT OF SENATOR HATCH

Senator HATCH. Thank you, Mr. Chairman. I am happy to do that. It was a real battle in my office between the generic industry and the pharmaceutical industry, the pharma companies. And at one point they both jumped up, all three of them, and decided to bolt out of the office. And two of them, they got to the door and two of them got at the same time and got stuck in the door.

[Laughter.]

We all started to laugh so I said come on back, and they came back, but there was one point when I said I am going to kill both of you.

[Laughter.]

There were three, but two of them were particularly bad, and I really got really irritated. I had a bad tooth at the time, and that aggravated it as well.

[Laughter.]

But to make a long story short, we have been very pleased with the efficacy of Hatch-Waxman, and Henry deserves a lot of credit at that time for cooperating on this.

At the inception of the Generic Drug Users Fee Program in October 2012, there were approximately 2,800 generic applications awaiting approval, and the average approval time for an application was, if I got it right, 30 months. Going into its 4th year and the $1.2 billion later, the backlog has increased to 4,000 plus applications, and the average approval time for an application has steadily risen from 30 months in fiscal year 2011, 43 months in fiscal year 2014, to 48 months in fiscal year 2015. This is eight times longer than the statutory 6-month review time called for by the Hatch-Waxman Act, of which it is one of the bills that I feel very pleased about.

Further, since 2013, the number of approvals show a declining trend in overall approvals, both tentative and final. FDA approved 619 generics in 2012, 535 in 2013, 500 in 2014, and 346 in fiscal year 2015. A critical subset of approvals are first generics. First generics offer the first opportunity for consumers to benefit from the savings provided by generic drugs over brand drugs but only if they are approved on the first earliest day. As I understand it, it is staggering to think of the savings that were lost in the U.S. health care system in 2015 alone due to first generic approval delays.

Having said all that, I want to personally thank you for the work that you do. You do a terrific job, and I recognize it. But would you agree that this backlog keeps safe, low-cost generic drugs off the market and reduces competition? Just yes or no.

Dr. WOODCOCK. Yes.

Senator HATCH. Yes, I thought you would. Let me go a little bit farther. Will the backlog be eliminated before the start of GDUFA II?

Dr. WOODCOCK. Absolutely.

Senator HATCH. You think it will be?

Dr. WOODCOCK. We have already acted on 82 percent of—at least communicated with the company on 82 percent of those.

Senator HATCH. OK. How many applications of first generic products has the agency received since GDUFA was implemented?

Dr. WOODCOCK. That I do not know.

Senator HATCH. That is OK. Would you provide that to us?

Dr. WOODCOCK. Yes. We can get back to you. It is about 15 percent of the workload, and we expedite all those.

Senator HATCH. I appreciate that. How many first generic applications have missed approval on the earliest possible date over the last, say, 3 years if you have that knowledge?

Dr. WOODCOCK. I will have to get back to you on that, too.

Senator HATCH. You will get back to us?

Dr. WOODCOCK. It is a small number, though.

Senator HATCH. OK. Will you submit for the record the target action dates for the first generics pending before the agency without naming the applicant and the associated reference products? That would help us up here.

Dr. WOODCOCK. Yes. We can do that.

Senator HATCH. OK. How does FDA track prioritization of generic applications such as those associated with public health needs, drug shortages, or first generics? And what is the average approval time for these critical applications?

Dr. WOODCOCK. We track them through our new IT system where—and we have project management over all these applications now. We have a project manager aware of each one of them and making sure it moves properly through the system.

Senator HATCH. OK.

Dr. WOODCOCK. And we can get you the numbers.

Senator HATCH. Thank you. My time is expired.

Mr. Chairman, may I make kind of a statement here at the end?

The CHAIRMAN. Yes.

Senator HATCH. The reason Hatch-Waxman was so essential is because there were only about 16 to 18 percent of generics on the marketplace back when we did that. Today, it is approaching 90 percent. And that has been a very, very good thing. However, some people have played the market, too, and have distorted it even with regard to generics. So we want to get to the bottom of this.

I personally want to thank the Chairman and Ranking Member of this committee for getting into this, and I intend to help them every step of the way.

I also want to personally thank the people at FDA. It is a hard job. You have all kinds of pressure on you. There are all kinds of irritations and comments and screaming and shouting about these things, and we do not give you enough help to do it.

I also was the author of the FDA Revitalization Act and getting you the huge facility that you have out there where there have been 30 plus offices all over this area. All I can say is that I hope you will keep going because the generics are absolutely critical to this country and absolutely critical to our Federal budget and absolutely critical to the successful quotient and reputation of the FDA. Hopefully, if you see any changes in Hatch-Waxman or other bills that you are subject to that you think would help, we would sure like to hear from you.

Dr. WOODCOCK. Absolutely.

Senator HATCH. OK. Thank you, Mr. Chairman.

The CHAIRMAN. Thanks, Senator Hatch.

And before we go to Senator Murphy, I may have made a misstatement earlier, Dr. Woodcock. I said that there were no generic drugs 30 years ago. There were some——

Dr. WOODCOCK. Right.

Senator HATCH. There were some.

The CHAIRMAN [continuing]. Right, but they had to go through the whole process. What would be the accurate way to describe the percent of generic drugs 30 years ago?

Dr. WOODCOCK. I believe there were some. They were not well uptaken because they had quality problems as well. So the program that was put into place improved the quality and acceptability of them as well, but there were some generic drugs out there at that time.

The CHAIRMAN. OK.

Senator Murphy.

STATEMENT OF SENATOR MURPHY

Senator MURPHY. Thank you very much, Mr. Chairman. Welcome, Dr. Woodcock.

Dr. WOODCOCK. Thank you.

Senator MURPHY. Thank you for your service.

A comment and one question: The comment is just an extension on the point that Senator Warren was making. I am hopeful that we are going to spend some serious time and attention to this question of spiraling drug costs important for consumers. It is certainly important for the Federal budget.

But I would agree with Senator Warren that I also hope that we will not place too great a share of the blame on the regulatory process. There are certainly efficiencies that we can gain, but I agree with her, and I think it is worth restating that what is exceptional about the United States is the way in which we have structured our market for drugs, the way in which prices are set. We are virtually the only country in the world that does not have a process for capping and controlling drug costs. The result of that is that American consumers and the U.S. Government bear the lion's share of R&D costs for the entire industry globally, and the rest of the world's consumers are free riders.

Second, and more difficult to talk about, is the fact that if you take a look at the 16 publicly traded companies that sell the best-selling drugs in this country, half of them are taking in a greater profit at the end of the year than they are spending on research and development. And that is 2014 numbers. We certainly have discovered and dispensed life-changing drugs because of the profit motive built into our system, but those are pretty stunning numbers.

My question is a very specific one. You, I think, ended your testimony with a set of challenges and barriers, and one of those that you outlined was this problem in which we do not have a convincing bioequivalence test method available. And I think that is worth just exploring a little bit. You have money to try to develop those pathways, and so you also caution us that it takes time. So can you tell us a little bit more about the timing of that research, how we should judge its effectiveness?

And then to the extent that we have been successful in getting another $2 billion over in NIH, what is the degree of cooperation with NIH? What more can they be doing to try to solve this problem?

Dr. WOODCOCK. Thank you. NIH does not typically do this type of research. This is very applied research. And what we are talking about here is that drugs that are not systemically absorbed and go through the blood are hard to determine whether they are bioequivalent to the innovator drug. So that would be all the creams and lotions and different topical agents, as well as inhalation drugs. And then we have a new category of very complicated drugs out there that also are going to pose problems in characterizing them and making sure they are the same as the innovator, kind of similar to the biosimilars problem.

The research we are doing, I think you can judge if it is going to bear fruit because we would issue draft guidance, and the draft guidance would have a new bioequivalence test in it. And we might do workshops before that and other things to get the scientific community on board. But we would say instead of having to do a clinical trial and all that entails, a comparative clinical trial, you can use this bioequivalence test. And you put the cream on these people and you put the cream on maybe their other arm or whatever and then you measure something or whatever you do, whatever we say, and then that would stand in for the bioequivalence results. And that would really improve uptake and generic competition in these areas where they are not systemically absorbed drugs.

Senator MURPHY. And just forgive my ignorance, but these guidances would be for classes of drugs, types of treatments, or for specific drugs or treatments?

Dr. WOODCOCK. It would probably be for drug classes sometimes and for specific drugs other times.

Senator MURPHY. Do you have enough funding to get to where you think we should be 5 years from now or 10 years from now in terms of the amount of guidance necessary to keep up with the pace of technological change on these drugs?

Dr. WOODCOCK. I would have to get back to you on that. We have invested a substantial amount, although compared to NIH or something, we have invested about $24 million. We are having a lot of research done, but it takes time, as I said in my testimony, to get that research finished to understand the implications, translate it into policy and guidance, and then educate the world on how to do these studies.

But this is the key to some of that silver gap there of drugs that do not have generic competition at all——

Senator MURPHY. Right.

Dr. WOODCOCK [continuing]. Because it is too expensive or almost impossible or infeasible for them to figure out how to show they are the same.

Senator MURPHY. Great. Thank you very much, Mr. Chairman. Thank you, Dr. Woodcock.

The CHAIRMAN. Senator Whitehouse.

STATEMENT OF SENATOR WHITEHOUSE

Senator WHITEHOUSE. Thank you, Chairman. Thank you, Dr. Woodcock, for being here. I will continue on this same theme.

I am not an advocate for government price controls, but it does seem to me that there are circumstances in which very clever people have either observed or created a monopoly for themselves and then used that monopoly power to extort prices that the market would not support if it were actually operating correctly.

And it seems to me that there are some pretty obvious signals of when that might be taking place. To me, it is not a determinative factor, but it is a red flag factor. If the people involved are not in the business of creating pharmaceuticals but they are in the business of speculation, that ought to put up a red flag to me. If the price hike is beyond a certain amount, let us say 1,000 percent, again, not fully determinative but that maybe should send up a little red flag. If there are no alternatives to which a certain set of customers or patients can readily turn——

Dr. WOODCOCK. Right.

Senator WHITEHOUSE [continuing]. That would seem to be part of the monopoly posture. And I am wondering if your organization is looking in any way at trying to define where the market failure is taking place and saying, OK, these are red flags or if you see that as somebody else's job?

Dr. WOODCOCK. The report issued yesterday by HHS on some of the pricing issues around pharmaceuticals gets to some of those issues. And for the economic ones, I believe that they are better suited than the FDA because, as I said, we are doctors, not——

Senator WHITEHOUSE. So the FDA is not looking at that?

Dr. WOODCOCK. We look at sole source because that is a red flag that there could be a shortage because there is only one manufacturer and if something goes wrong, that is a big problem.

Senator WHITEHOUSE. You are looking at it from a shortage point of view as opposed to a price manipulation point of view?

Dr. WOODCOCK. That is right.

Senator WHITEHOUSE. OK.

Dr. WOODCOCK. If you could show the bar chart. Yes.

[Slide.]

We look at those that have few competitors so some of the ones in that chart where they only have one generic, that might be the only drug on the market actually. The innovator may be off or there are only two or there are two. Those are areas where there is not a lot of competition and where there could be a shortage or a loss of product.

Senator WHITEHOUSE. It just strikes me that if we can correctly define the characteristics of the bad behavior that everybody on this committee sees and acknowledges exists, then going the long way around to trying to figure out how your drug approval process can resolve that problem is a very inefficient way to do it. You should go right at where the problem is, which I think is speculators buy drugs that do not have competition and who create massive price increases. And if you simply said we are not going to allow that any longer, then people go away and they go find more productive things to do with their time.

Let me ask you a different question entirely. We have had conversations about the device-regulating side of the FDA and about the drug-regulating side of the FDA and about the need for there to be a new track in the FDA for drug device combinations. And this committee is obviously looking at that. What can you tell me about where the FDA is in terms of making a recommendation to us on what the drug-device combination would look like? What is your recommendation to us for that?

Dr. WOODCOCK. I believe that the FDA is ready to work with the committee on this, and we are very interested in looking at some solutions to this problem.

Senator WHITEHOUSE. Have you proposed any?

Dr. WOODCOCK. I do not know that we have proposed specific legislation, and I do not know where the administration is on that. However, I would say from my own technical point of view that it is a problem. We need more clarity and we need a different path that——

Senator WHITEHOUSE. Both you in charge of the drug side and the device side have said the same thing to me, which is you cannot do drug-device combinations using our process. There has got be a new process that emerges. So do you think it would be wise for you and the device side to sit down and spend a little time making a recommendation to us as to how you think those drug-device combinations might be best regulated?

Dr. WOODCOCK. Certainly. We have had numerous conversations about this with our colleagues at devices and the Office of Combination Products and gone through multiple scenarios. I think we would be very eager to discuss it with the committee.

Senator WHITEHOUSE. A proposal from the agency that would actually be obliged to implement it, I think, would be helpful to the committee.

Thank you, Chairman.

The CHAIRMAN. Thank you, Senator Whitehouse.

Senator Murray, do you have any further comment?

Senator MURRAY. I do not have any further questions. I just want to thank Dr. Woodcock for her really important expertise in your answer to your questions. I think this has been an excellent hearing. We have a lot of work ahead of us, and I look forward to working with you on a bipartisan fashion to move forward. Thank you.

The CHAIRMAN. Thank you, Senator Murray.

And let me add my thanks to you, Dr. Woodcock. You have been there 30 years in one position or another, but it is hard to imagine there would be a more exciting time than right now, given the rate of innovation.

We have the logical tension that exists between prices, safety, effectiveness, and then incentivizing and encouraging a supply of new treatments and cures and devices that will save lives. We are talking about the next generation of cancer treatments and innovative therapies for ALS and Alzheimer's, infectious diseases. We have seen what has happened with hepatitis C. We have seen what has happened with cystic fibrosis. You have had a role in all of that. We are told that in Alzheimer's that if we simply delayed onset for 5 years, that could save our health care system $367 billion by 2015, and the grief and the anguish is incalculable. And there have been 123 unsuccessful attempts at developing drugs for Alzheimer's, I am told, while only four are successful.

So my hope at least is that while we are working on safe and effective and keeping the market competitive so prices are as low as possible, that we do not do anything to discourage or dis-incent the development of these new lifesaving treatments.

The hearing record will remain open for 10 days. Members may submit additional information if they would like.

The next session in our committee will be an executive session on February 9 to begin the step-by-step process to produce legislation. There will be several bills considered with amendments. These are all bipartisan bills in that sense that they have been sponsored by members of our committee on both sides of the aisle. And perhaps they can grow into companion legislation to the work that 21st Century Cures package that the House has already passed.

The President is vitally interested in what we are doing with precision medicine and also now with his cancer initiatives. We welcome the Administration's input on that.

We look forward to February 9, and we thank you, Dr. Woodcock, for coming today. The committee will stand adjourned.

[Editor's Note: Response to questions submitted by the committee were not available at time of print.]

39

[Whereupon, at 11:31 a.m., the hearing was adjourned.]

○